The Frans Hals Museum
Haarlem

D0487129

Antoon Erftemeijer
Henriëtte Fuhri Snethlage
Neeltje Köhler

THE FRANS HALS MUSEUM
HAARLEM

Ludion

Museum of the Golden Age. This is how the Frans Hals Museum describes itself – and the description is by no means an exaggeration. The museum has an inestimably valuable collection of paintings – some of the greatest masterpieces of the 17th century – by Frans Hals (the civic guard works), Jan Steen, Jan de Bray, Johannes Verspronck, Pieter Saenredam and many other Dutch Old Masters. It owns hundreds of such masterpieces, which are displayed in changing exhibitions.

And there is much more to the museum than the collection alone. The Frans Hals Museum owes its unique character in part to the building in which it is housed: an Old Men's Alms House dating from the 17th century. With its picturesque gatehouse, elegant courtyard and galleries with beamed ceilings, this magnificent building provides the perfect ambiance for the paintings. A visit to this museum is a visit to the Golden Age. The atmosphere of the times is enhanced by stained glass, furniture and other decorative objects, which are displayed throughout the galleries.

It is no coincidence that such an important collection of 17th-century Dutch art is to be found in Haarlem. For half a century – from around 1580 to 1630 – Haarlem was the acknowledged centre of painting in the Republic of the United Provinces. Before Amsterdam made a name for itself, the art of the Golden Age was flourishing in Haarlem. It was there that several typical 17th-century genres first developed.

The art of the Golden Age did not appear out of a clear blue sky. Haarlem had important painters like Geertgen tot St Jans and Jan Mostaert in the Middle Ages. But it was in the 16th century that a number of very talented artists appeared on the scene, artists who – importantly – looked beyond the country's borders to the art of other nations. Jan van Scorel was one of them. His paintings, like those of his pupil Maerten van Heemskerck, show how Dutch painting gradually modernized, influenced primarily by the Italian Renaissance. Their art is well represented in the Frans Hals Museum.

Haarlem did not stand still. When a transition occurred in art – in Italy and elsewhere – which dealt more freely and experimentally with composition, form and colour, Holland joined in, with Haarlem in the lead. Artists like Cornelis Cornelisz van Haarlem, Hendrick Goltizus and Karel van Mander have gone down in history as the Haarlem Mannerists. In their sometimes massive canvases and panels, depicting subjects from the Bible and classical antiquity, the virtuoso painted nudes, playing their appointed roles in amazing poses, are particularly striking.

Whereas the Haarlem Mannerists, working around the end of the 16th century, were still primarily followers, the picture changed around 1600. A number of painters in Haarlem struck out in what was then an essentially new direction, with works usually of 'parlour size': still lifes, landscapes, seascapes and 'modern pictures' (scenes of everyday life). Realistic tableaux, albeit not infrequently with a moral lesson incorporated in them: 'earthly riches are transient', 'moderation in all things' – messages like this were put across with more or less explicit symbols.

The 'new art' focused on a new market. The Roman Catholic church had largely ceased to function as a major patron in the Protestant United Provinces. True, official bodies and institutions still awarded numerous commissions, but never before had the 'ordinary citizen' been dominant in the art market on such a scale. At local markets and auctions, from the painters in their studios, through art dealers and lotteries: the millions of paintings the Dutch painters produced reached the general public by many different routes. And it was not only the wealthy who bought them: virtually everyone had art at home.

It was by specializing that the painters succeeded in making an unprecedented artistic breakthrough. Still lifes with fish, Italianate landscapes, coastal views, winter landscapes: the Frans Hals Museum has magnificent examples of paintings of these and other endlessly repeated but always revitalized subjects. Examples that have been collected by the city over the course of several centuries by way of commissions, purchases, gifts or in other ways. Since 1913 they have been exhibited in the historic building in Groot Heiligland, which has now been converted so that it meets the latest criteria for a museum. Numerous art lovers from the Netherlands and abroad visit the museum again and again. The Frans Hals Museum hopes and endeavours to meet as far as possible their desire to relive something of the Golden Age.

Karel Schampers
Director, Frans Hals Museum

1598	The Haarlem town council decides to build an old men's alms house.
1606	A grand gala of the *rederijkers* or rhetorical societies is held to finance the construction of the old men's home.
1607	A great lottery is organized for the same purpose. The draw lasted 52 days and nights; each draw was accompanied by the reading of a verse that had been submitted and a drum roll.
1609	On 1 February the first residents move into the Old Men's Alms House. The men's accommodation was built around a courtyard; two men lived in each cottage.
1664	Frans Hals paints the portraits of the regents and regentesses who governed the Old Men's Alms House. These trustees were accountable to the town council. The day-to-day running of the home was the responsibility of a housefather and a housemother. The portraits of the trustees can now be seen in the museum.
1810	The old men move to the Proveniershuis in the Grote Houtstraat. The building becomes an orphanage; 127 orphans aged from four to 18 move in. Attics are opened up to create space for dormitories.
1854	The orphanage becomes the property of the Reformed Church. The trustees are now appointed by the parish council. A housefather and housemother run the place on a daily basis. They are assisted by a seamstress, a schoolmaster and a nursemaid. They all live in the orphanage.
1858	Two classrooms are built in the east wing. Children from the town can also attend lessons there. The orphans go to school until they turn 14. The girls are trained as seamstresses. When they are 18, a position is found for them. The boys are usually apprenticed to a crafts-man and then go out to work.
1908	The orphans move to a new building in the Olieslagerslaan, which is cheaper to maintain. The economic malaise in the 19th century had had an impact on the finances of the orphan-age. There was a constant shortage of money. If essential building works were not post-poned, only the absolute minimum was done. Rooms were damp, airless and too small.
1908–1913	In 1908 Haarlem town council purchases the building to house the city's art collection. Large parts of the building are demolished and rebuilt in early 17th-century style to a design by L.C. Dumont, the municipal architect. The original floor plan, the entrance gate and the main building with the Renaissance hall, the trustees' rooms and the chapel are preserved.
1913	The museum opens on 13 May 1913. It is named after Haarlem's most famous artist, Frans Hals.

1581	The States of Holland award Haarlem all the goods of the Catholic convents, monasteries and similar institutions in the city. The 'gift' is meant as restitution for the losses suffered during the revolt against Catholic Spain.
1590–1593	Cornelis Cornelisz van Haarlem is commissioned by the City of Haarlem to paint four works for the Prinsenhof, part of the town hall. They are *The Marriage of Peleus and Thetis* (p 29), *The Fall* (now in the Rijksmuseum, Amsterdam*), The Massacre of the Innocents* (pp 26–27) and *The Monk and the Beguine* (p 28). Three of the four are still in the city's collection (now the Frans Hals Museum).
1620	The town council buys Hendrick Pot's *Triumph of Prince William of Orange.*
1622	An inventory of the Prinsenhof drawn up in this year lists, among other things, Jan van Scorel's *Pilgrims to Jerusalem* (pp 16–17), Maerten van Heemskerck's *St Luke painting the Madonna* (p 19), and many other artistic treasures.
1625	The last brother in the important Jansklooster in the Jansstraat dies. Some of the works of art in this monastery pass into the city's possession, among them Van Scorel's *Baptism in the Jordan* (p 18) and Pieter Pietersz's *The Three Youths in the Fiery Furnace* (p 30).
1630	The town council commissions Pieter de Grebber to paint *The German Emperor grants the Sword to the Arms of Haarlem.*
1800–1825	Nine militia paintings are brought to safety in the town hall, after the abolition of the civic guard in 1797. They had been damaged on several occasions in the great hall of the Cluveniersdoelen, where they had hung until this time. Four of the nine are by Frans Hals; the city had already acquired a fifth militia work by Hals at the end of the 17th century.
1862	Official opening to the public of a 'Municipal Museum' in the town hall. One hundred and twenty-three paintings are exhibited, and a catalogue is published. The collection has mean-while grown as a result of gifts from private individuals and a major loan (19 items) by St Eliza-beth's Hospital. Impressionists and their contemporaries visit the museum to study and copy Hals: Monet, Cassatt, Liebermann, Whistler, Sargent and many more.
1875	Foundation of the Association to Expand the Collection of Art and Antiquities, which will aug-ment the museum collection with dozens of old masters.
1913	Opening of the Frans Hals Museum in the Old Men's Alms House in Groot Heiligland, to which the municipal museum collection is moved. Since then the collection has grown as a result of bequests (among them the H.J.D.D. Enschedé bequest in 1941), purchases, loans, gifts and the support of the Association of Friends of the Frans Hals Museum.

Triptych depicting the Birth,
Crucifixion and Resurrection of Christ,
c. 1515

Hans Memling, follower of
c. 1433–1499 (?)
Panel, centre 96 x 72 cm,
side panels 99.5 x 34.5 cm

An extremely fine painted altarpiece, part of the museum's small
but nonetheless important collection of medieval paintings. The side
panels depict the birth of Christ
(left) and his resurrection from the
grave (right). In the centre is his crucifixion on Golgotha, the 'place of
the skull' just outside Jerusalem.
The city painted in the background
springs from the artist's imagina-
tion. Christ is already dead: to make
sure of his death 'one of the soldiers
with a spear pierced his side; and
forthwith came there out blood
and water' (John 19, 34). Christ's
mother mourns at the lower left;
at the lower right soldiers throw
dice for Christ's garments.

The triptych is regarded as the
work of a follower of the Southern
Netherlandish painter Hans Memling. It may be a copy of a lost work
by Memling.

The Benedictine Saints Boniface,
Gregory the Great,
Adalbert of Egmond
and Jerome of Noordwijk, c. 1529/30

Jan Joesten van Hillegom
c. 1475–after 1535
Panel, 124 x 138 cm

Four saints pose in monks' habits. These are medieval saints. The habits are those of the Benedictine order. Boniface (*c.* 675–754) (left), with bishop's mitre, crosier and book of the gospels, was murdered while undertaking missionary work in Dokkum. Next to him stands Pope Gregory the Great (*c.* 540–604), who wrote the life of St Benedict, the founder of the order. Turning towards him is the preacher Adalbert (?–741), who assisted Willibrord in missionary work in North Holland. Jerome of Noordwijk, lastly, was a missionary in West Friesland a century later, and was murdered by the Normans (hence the sword).

This large work is actually two connected paintings on panels, each bearing two figures. Originally they were the outer panels of the wings of an altar screen. The inner panels depicted four female saints (now in the Koninklijke Musea in Brussels). The whereabouts of the central panel are unknown. The altarpiece was probably made for the Benedictine Abbey in Egmond, where Adelbert was buried. The work may have been painted by Jan Joesten van Hillegom, who lived and worked in the abbey for some time in the 16th century.

The Egyptian hermit St Anthony (c. 251–356) is sunk in prayer. Around him, all sorts of diabolical beings try to tempt him away from his piety. At the upper left he is even dragged viciously up into the air. However, he is unmoved by it all, according to the surviving contemporary account of his life by St Athanasius. Anthony withstood the many demonic trials and survived to the age of 105. He was venerated for centuries as the patron saint who gave protection against contagious diseases. He is also regarded as the founding father of the monastic life. Jan Mandijn, who was born in Haarlem but worked in Antwerp, drew his inspiration for this work from a painting of the same name by Hieronymus Bosch (c. 1450–1516), which is now in Lisbon.

A large panel and a puzzling scene. In a mountainous region naked people with primitive weapons fight soldiers with firearms, halberds and a cannon. The painting was rediscovered in 1909, and recognized as the work by Jan Mostaert that was described by his biographer Karel van Mander in 1604: 'There is also a Landscape, being in West India, with many naked people ...' which was 'left unfinished'.

Now, however, the work does not appear unfinished; possibly it was completed later. It is hard to say what the scene means. It may indeed relate to an event in 'West India', or in other words America. It could depict an incident during an expedition of conquest by the Spaniard Vásquez de Coronado in Southwestern America (Arizona). The painting may have been intended as a condemnation of atrocities

committed by the Conquistadors. It
is also possible that the panel has
a more general meaning: the virtu-
ous idyllic society of 'noble savages'
resists the evil of the modern world.
The painting may thus have been
meant to encourage good behaviour
and warn against a cruel desire for
conquest.

*Group Portrait of Pilgrims
of the Knightly Brotherhood
of the Holy Land in Haarlem,
c.1528*

Jan van Scorel 1495–1562
Panel, 114 x 275.7 cm

Twelve pious men, ranged two
by two in a procession, with palm
fronds in their hands. They are
members of the Haarlem 'Jerusalem
Brotherhood'. Everyone who had
visited the Holy Sepulchre in
Jerusalem could become a member
of the brotherhood. Societies like
this were also to be found in other
towns and cities. On the left, the servant of the brotherhood shows the
Sepulchre in a small painting within
the painting. The second man from
the left carries two palm fronds: he
had made the pilgrimage to far-off
Jerusalem twice. Under the portraits, edifying verses provide infor-
mation about the people and the
year of their pilgrimage. The third
person from the right is the painter
Van Scorel himself. This almost
three-metre-wide panel with its
realistic, carefully painted heads is
one of the oldest group portraits in
Northern Netherlandish art.

'And it came to pass in those days that Jesus came from Nazareth of Galilee, and was baptized of John in Jordan. And straightway coming up out of the water, he saw the heavens opened, and the Spirit like a dove descending upon him' (Mark 1, 9–10). It is this New Testament story that Van Scorel has illustrated here. To the left of centre stands the Jewish preacher John the Baptist. Jesus sits under the tree. The dove flies to the right of the tree. In creating this scene, Van Scorel was clearly inspired by works by Italian masters of his time, among them Giorgione (the landscape) and Raphael (the three male figures on the right). Van Scorel spent the years 1520 to 1524 in Italy. He was even curator of the Vatican art collection for a while, so that he became very familiar with modern Italian painting. He painted this work for the important Haarlem monastery, the Commanderij van St Jan, on his return from Italy.

For centuries Luke the Evangelist was the patron saint of painters and their guilds. He had after all, according to medieval legend, actually painted Mary and the infant Jesus. Many painters honoured him with a 'portrait'. In this work a man stands behind Luke. According to a contemporary explanation, he represents poetic inspiration: with his right hand he guides the painter's hand. The *trompe l'oeil cartellino* nailed up at the lower left states among other things, 'This painting is given as a keepsake by Maerten van Heemskerck, who made it. He did this in honour of St Luke; he also had us, his guild brothers, in his thoughts'. The work was thus given by the painter to his guild brothers, in all likelihood shortly before he set off on a trip to Rome, and was probably intended to be hung in the Church of St Bavo in the Grote Markt. Given the strikingly low vantage point – the painting should be viewed from below – it must have been designed for a high position: above the altar or on a column.

Triptych with Ecce Homo, 1559–60

Maerten van Heemskerck 1498–1574
Panel, centre 218.5 x 150 cm;
side panels 218.5 x 67 cm

In the centre panel of this substantial triptych a tortured Jesus stands between the Roman governor Pontius Pilate (right) and two executioners. Jesus was accused of blasphemy. Pilate presents the tortured but, according to Pilate, innocent prisoner to a group of Jews with the words, 'Behold the man' (in Latin 'Ecce homo'). High priests and their followers demand crucifixion. Eventually, Pilate gives in to them. Van Heemskerck leaves out the Jews: the viewers are thus confronted more directly with Jesus's suffering and as it were form the crowd themselves. The side panels depict the donors, with their patron saints Christopher (left) and Martha (right). The triptych belongs with Heemskerck's triptych 'The Entombment' (now in Brussels): they originally hung together in a Delft church or monastery. These passion retables may have been donated by people who survived the plague epidemic that ravaged Delft in 1557–58. A recent restoration revealed that there was originally much more blood on Jesus's body.

ECCE HOMO   1 5 5 9

Side panels of the Drapers' altar:
outside the Annunciation,
inside the Adoration of the Shepherds
and the Adoration of the Magi,
1546–47

Maerten Jacobsz van Heemskerck
1498–1574
Panel, each 261.5 x 122.5 cm

Maerten van Heemskerck made
these two side panels for the Haarlem Guild of Drapers, the guild of
the cloth and wool weavers. The
panels were intended for the Guild
of Drapers' altar, which was in the
Great Church, otherwise known as
the Church of St Bavo. They were
probably added to an existing centrepiece, whose whereabouts are
now unknown.

    When closed, the two side pan-
els show the Annunciation to the
Virgin Mary. Mary kneels at her
prayer stool, with a Bible open
before her. While the magnificently
attired Archangel Gabriel tells her
of the birth of Jesus, the dove of
the Holy Ghost descends on Mary.
Mary's robe must originally have
been blue. The smalt, the pigment
that Van Heemskerck used for her
garments, has faded over the centuries, and only the brown of the
binder now remains.

    Open, the panels show the Ado-
ration of the Shepherds on the left
and the Adoration of the Magi on
the right. Maerten van Heemskerck
has made a place for himself among
the magi and their retinue. He is
the man with the beard, to the right
of the standing magus. The city
acquired the side panels in 1581.
In 1591 Cornelis van Haarlem was
commissioned to paint a new centre
panel depicting the Massacre of the
Innocents (pp 26–27).

Between 1590 and 1593 the painter Cornelis Cornelisz van Haarlem received a major and honourable commission from the town council to paint four large works, *The Massacre of the Innocents*, *A Monk and a Beguine*, *The Marriage of Peleus and Thetis* and *The Fall*. The paintings were to hang in the Prinsenhof, in the former Dominican monastery. The Prinsenhof lay just behind the town hall and was used as a guest house for the stadholders. The choice of subjects for the four paintings was undoubtedly related to their destination. They warned against discord, temptation and taking wrong decisions. The stories depicted come from the Old Testament (*The Fall*), the New Testament (*The Massacre*), mythology (*The Marriage of Peleus and Thetis*) and the (legendary) history of Haarlem (*A Monk and a Beguine*).

The *Massacre* was to be the new centrepiece for two side panels by Maerten van Heemskerck (pp 22–23). Until 1581 these panels had hung in the Great Church, otherwise known as the Church of St Bavo, over the altar of the Drapers. After the Reformation they became the property of the city. The entry for the purchase of linen 'so that a painting by master Cornelis might be made upon it' has been preserved in the treasurer's accounts. The payment to Cornelis van Haarlem is also recorded. In 1591 he received 600 pounds for 'his work and art in making and painting a certain large scene of the killing of the children by King Herod...' and for the painting of *A Monk and a Beguine*. Two years later, in 1593, Cornelis van Haarlem was paid a further 600 pounds for *The Marriage of Peleus and Thetis* and *The Fall* (now in the Rijksmuseum in Amsterdam).

The Massacre of the Innocents, 1591	Cornelis Cornelisz van Haarlem 1562–1638 Canvas, 268 x 257 cm

'Here one sees a great confusion of naked Child-killers, and the efforts of the Mothers to save their children: also divers Flesh tones of different ages, thus of Men, Women, and that tender young flesh of the children, and the change wrought by death in the drained bodies.' So wrote the artist's biographer Karel van Mander in his *SchilderBoeck* of 1604. He described the work as 'an excellent piece'.

The painting depicts the horrific massacre in Bethlehem that was carried out on the orders of the tyrannical King Herod in an attempt to kill the newborn Christ child (Matthew 2:16–18). In a turbulent composition, the callous soldiers of Herod's army seize the helpless infants. Women trying in vain to save their children are thrown roughly to the ground by the soldiers.

Cornelis van Haarlem painted this work for Haarlem town council. It was intended as a new centre panel to two side panels that had been painted by Maerten van Heemskerck in 1564 (pp 22–23). Cornelis van Haarlem made the side panels – which were originally lobed – rectangular, and filled in the corners so that it appears as if

Maerten van Heemskerck's work carries through. To express his admiration for his distinguished predecessor, he used a study drawing for the arm of the soldier on the right in the painting from one of Van Heemskerck's sketchbooks, which he owned. The triptych was to hang in the Prinsenhof, the stadholders' guest quarters.

A monk squeezes a nun's breast. The explanation most often given of this picture is that it is a 16th-century satire on the dissolute lives of those living in cloisters: monks and nuns were frequently accused of drunkenness, gluttony, avarice and licentious behaviour. The wine and the fruit would therefore allude to an immoral life.

In old museum catalogues, however, the subject of this painting is described as 'the miracle of Haarlem'. According to the legend, a Haarlem nun was accused of having concealed a pregnancy and birth. It was believed that her motherhood could be detected by squeezing her breast: if milk was expressed, the accusation was true. The painting depicts the moment when a monk 'experienced in the medical sciences' squeezes the nun's breast. This is when the miracle occurred: it was not milk, but wine that flowed from her breast. This proved the nun's piety and innocence. In this case the wine and fruit symbolize a virginal life. Which explanation is the correct one remains the question.

A story from classical antiquity. All the gods were invited to the wedding of Peleus, the son of the King of Greece, and the sea goddess Thetis, except for Eris, the goddess of strife and discord. She took her revenge by sowing dissent. Uninvited, she appeared at the wedding feast and threw a golden apple bearing the inscription 'for the fairest' among the numerous wedding guests.

Vulcan, the god of blacksmiths, sits in the foreground and drains the last dregs of wine from a pitcher. Behind him lies his hammer. On the left in the foreground sits the shepherd god Pan, identified by his large ears, little horns and goatee beard, and his Pan pipes. On the right sits a group of nymphs making music. Their music making expresses harmony. On the left under the trees, Apollo, the patron of the arts, plays a violin. In the background on the left, the uninvited Eris flies away from the party.

Precisely in the centre of the painting, Zeus sits at a table with the disputed apple in his hand. Three goddesses, Venus, Juno and Minerva, believed that they had a claim to the fruit. Paris, a Trojan prince, was given the unenviable task of deciding between them. This moment is illustrated at the upper right in the painting. Paris chose Venus, who offered him the beautiful Helen in return. His choice had disastrous consequences since it led indirectly to the Trojan War.

The painting was intended for the Prinsenhof in Haarlem and warns against discord and wrong decisions.

Pieter Pietersz 1539/41–1603
Panel, 222.8 x 182.2 cm

This crowded, complex composition illustrates an Old Testament story: three youths in the fiery furnace (Daniel 3). A golden image towers over the scene. On the left a crowd kneels in worship before it, apart from three young Hebrew men who are being taken prisoner. In the foreground they are being led away in manacles behind a chariot in which the Babylonian King Nebuchadnezzar rides in triumph. On the right is a fiery furnace in which the youths are to be burned to death.

However, 'the fire had no power over the men and they suffered nothing. Then the three men glorified and praised God from the furnace'. This awakened in Nebuchadnezzar great respect for the God of the Jews. Pieter Pietersz made this painting, in which an oven features prominently, for the Haarlem Guild of Bakers. It originally hung above the guild altar in the Church of St Bavo.

'And God said unto Noah, The end of all flesh is come before me; for the earth is filled with violence through them; and, behold, I will destroy them with the earth' we read in Genesis 6–8. Only Noah, his family and some animals were allowed to survive, by boarding an ark built by Noah out of gopher wood. Then 'the rain was upon the earth, forty days and forty nights'. This unfathomable tragedy of the Flood was depicted by many of the Mannerist painters: it was a challenge to the artist's ability to portray the human figure in contorted, dramatic poses. Van Mander was a master of the genre, as this little panel shows.

During the absence of their leader Moses and left without guidance, the Jewish people had a golden image of a calf made, so that they should nonetheless have 'gods, which shall go before us'. Burnt offerings were brought for the idol. And then the people 'sat down to eat and to drink, and rose up to play' (Exodus 32). The lapse was depicted by Karel van Mander in virtuoso style. In this dazzling Mannerist work, he succeeded in combining the atmospheric landscape tradition of Flemish art with modern Italian views on composition (for example, large figures at the side and dogs in the foreground). Van Mander painted this substantial canvas towards the end of his life.

Minerva, 1611	Hendrick Goltzius 1558–1617
	Canvas, 214 x 120 cm
Mercury, 1611	Canvas, 214 x 120 cm
Hercules and Cacus, 1613	Canvas, 207 x 142.5 cm

For centuries these three paintings of life-size nudes, the goddess Minerva, the god Mercury and the hero Hercules, have been an inseparable trio. And yet they were not all painted in the same year. Goltzius painted the *Minerva* and *Mercury* in 1611; the *Hercules and Cacus* followed in 1613, and may well have been commissioned by the Haarlem lawyer and town councillor Johan Colterman (*c.* 1565–1616), who probably had his 22-year-old son Johan Colterman Junior model for the young, powerful figure of Hercules. This painting is not quite the same size as the two earlier works, and its original frame was also slightly different. The earliest mention of the paintings hanging together dates from 1671, when they belonged to the daughter and son-in-law of Colterman Junior.

The three paintings together exemplify the humanist educational ideal. Theory (Mercury) and practice (Minerva) lead to skill and virtue. Virtue is personified in Hercules, who defeats the evil giant Cacus.

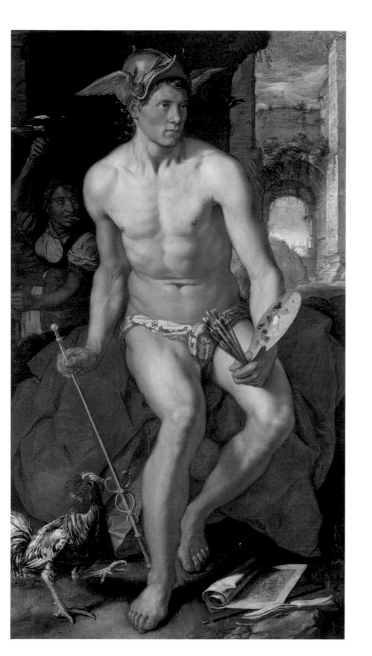

Minerva

Minerva is the goddess of wisdom and patron of the arts. She leans on her shield, which bears the head of Medusa. At her feet lie books, a folder, a pen and pen-holder, a weaver's shuttle and a lute: attributes that refer to the practice of the arts. Wisdom and stupidity are contrasted in this painting. King Midas with his ass's ears is notorious for his stupidity and his lack of judgement: in a musical contest, Midas chose the pipe music of the earthly Pan rather than the lyre playing of the divine Apollo. The Colosseum can be seen through an archway in the background.

Mercury

The mythological figure of Mercury was patron of the arts and god of rhetoric. He is recognizable by his winged helmet, the snake-entwined caduceus and a cockerel. In this version, his caduceus looks very much like a maulstick. At Mercury's feet lie drawing attributes, a set square, compasses, a drawing and an album of drawing patterns. Behind him stands a girl sticking her tongue out and holding a rattle and a magpie. In this painting, too, wisdom and stupidity are united: the girl symbolizes foolish prattle.

Hercules and Cacus

One of the labours of Hercules was to kill the fire-breathing giant Cacus. Cacus had stolen the cattle that Hercules was guarding. Hercules, identified by his lion skin and club, stands over the body of Cacus. He symbolizes the triumph of virtue over evil.

Hendrick Cornelisz Vroom
1562/63–1640
Canvas, 61 x 122.5 cm

Haarlem, city on the River Spaarne. This, at first sight, is what this painting is about. In the foreground the busy river, beyond it the walled city with the great Church of St Bavo in the centre and numerous other recognizable churches, monasteries and buildings. But the painting has another subject, too: the Haarlem brewer and burgomaster Johan Claesz Loo (c.1580–1660). He stands, swathed in an orange sash, in the bow of the sailing ship. His family coat of arms, a chevron and three fleurs-de-lis, can be seen on the small pennant flying at the stern. The masts of this vessel and of the small boat on the left, laden with barrels of beer, are both topped with a fleur-de-lis: this second vessel therefore also belonged to Loo. In other words, this painting, which he probably commissioned himself, is also a portrait of Loo, posing in front of his beloved city. Jacob Matham immortalized this same Loo and his possessions in a pen painting (p 61).

Arrival of Frederick V of the Palatinate
and Elizabeth Stuart in Vlissingen
on 29 April 1613, 1623

Hendrick Cornelisz Vroom
1562/63–1640
Canvas, 203 x 409 cm

One of the largest paintings in the
Frans Hals Museum: a view of Vlissingen, with numerous ships in the
foreground. It depicts the arrival
from England of the young newly-
weds Prince Frederick V of the
Palatinate and the English princess
Elizabeth Stuart. They made the
crossing on the 'Prince Royal'
(left of the centre), accompanied
by a fleet of English vessels. Princes
Maurice and Frederick Henry
formed the reception committee:
their Orange vessel lies in the centre
foreground. The newly married
couple are being rowed into the harbour aboard a fine sloop. They sub-
sequently continued their journey
to Heidelberg, where they were to
live. The event was a significant one
for the United Provinces: Frederick
V symbolized the Protestant cause
against the Spanish aggressor and
the Catholic inquisition. Holland,
after all, was still at war with Spain.
Shortly after this event, the United
Provinces signed a treaty with the
Union of Protestant German rulers.
Hendrick Vroom of Haarlem, who
painted this huge canvas, is regarded as the father of Dutch maritime
painting.

The Capture of Damiate, before 1628   Cornelis Claesz van Wieringen
                                          c. 1575–1633
                                          Canvas, 101 x 230 cm

A major event depicted on a grand scale: the capture of the Egyptian city of Damiate in the Nile Delta. This expedition was part of the fifth crusade (13th century), undertaken chiefly by Dutch and Frisian ships. The objective was to open up the route to Jerusalem. A vessel from Haarlem, recognizable by the (old) city arms, using a saw under the keel, succeeds in sawing through the chain that is shutting off the harbour. The notion that Haarlem played such a heroic role is now considered to be a myth – not least because it is technically extremely difficult to cut through a great harbour chain with a sailing ship. The painting was made for the headquarters of the Haarlem *Cluveniers* (civic guard), specifically to hang over the mantelpiece in the Council of War Chamber.

A fashionably dressed company hunts deer in the dunes. In the left foreground horsemen and beaters have two deer at bay. More or less in the centre of the painting, a small castle can be seen through the trees.

This is not a painting of an existing building or estate. In the 17th century, landscape paintings were painted 'from nature', but this did not mean that the paintings depicted real landscapes. Artists went out and drew parts of landscapes, then went back to their studios and constructed a new landscape from their various drawings. This means that in a painting a tree in Haarlem can grow next to a castle in Germany.

The subject of this painting, the deer hunt, was a device to liven up the landscape. At the same time this theme gives the painting a symbolic meaning. In the literature of the day, the deer hunt was often associated with the conquest of a woman. In his 'Amorum emblemata' (Emblems of Love) of 1608, for instance, Otto van Veen expressed it in verse thus:

Before you can capture a hart, you must first hunt love
By beseeching and adoring and paying court
The more pains it costs the more men desire it
What is easily captured is easily disdained

River Landscape with Ancient Tomb,
c. 1626

Cornelis Hendricksz Vroom
1591/92–1661
Panel, 29.5 x 60 cm

An Italianate landscape, centring on
the ruins of a tall, classical Roman
edifice, described as a tomb. Reliefs
on this building include a figure on
a throne and a horseman. The landscape is populated with various
human figures, some of whom
travel in a rowing boat along the
river in the foreground.

Vroom himself had most probably never been to Italy. He is likely
to have drawn his inspiration from
the work of colleagues, particularly
Adam Elsheimer and Jan van de
Velde. His ignorance of things Italian might explain the presence of
some very Dutch-looking plants
and trees, and the typically Dutch
motif of the woman knocking
acorns out of a tree for her pigs.

A shepherd and two shepherdesses
rest by a waterfall. They are in a
mountainous landscape, manifestly
not Dutch, through which a river
winds. On the right, a vista opens
out to a distant panorama. Mood
and atmosphere are the key in this
exceptionally fine painted panel.
It could be called idyllic or Arcadian,
but equally well (proto) Romantic.
The painter was a son, and probably
pupil, of the productive marine
painter Hendrick C. Vroom.
The Frans Hals Museum also
owns works by Hendrick. Initially,
Cornelis also painted marine subjects, but later he switched from
seascapes to landscapes. He is seen
as the trailblazer for the renowned
Jacob van Ruisdael.

While a mother and her child sit resting by the side of the road, a little group of peasants with two covered wagons passes by. The landscape is bathed in warm sunlight, and the atmosphere is one of great tranquility.

Pieter de Molijn was not concerned with painting a specific landscape, but with creating a mood: the sun shines, there are clouds – but not threatening ones – in the sky; in short, it is a peaceful day.

The artist has used several tried and tested tricks of the trade. The path is bathed in sunlight, for example, while the foreground and background are in shade, thus creating depth. He also used a composition of diagonals: the two paths that cross in the painting lead the eye into the distance.

Pieter de Molijn, born in London of Flemish parents, lived and worked in Haarlem, the cradle of the typical Dutch landscape in painting. He played a not insignificant part in the development of landscape as a genre. Around 1626 he became one of the first people to stress the creation of mood. Towards the middle of the 17th century, when he painted this work, this was still the fashion in landscape painting.

Mood and space are key in this typically Dutch river landscape conceived by Jan van Goyen in shades of brown. The church is probably based on the Church of St Lawrence in Alkmaar. For the rest, this appears to be an imaginary landscape; Van Goyen often mixed fantasy and reality. He was diligent in sketching from nature, and numerous drawings and sketches have survived. He painted landscapes in his studio, taking these studies from nature as his starting-point. There are hundreds of surviving paintings by him, usually coast and river views in brown tones, but he was not just prolific – his work was also of a high standard.

A small early work by the most famous landscape painter of the Golden Age. Jacob van Ruisdael probably painted it when he was in his early twenties. The size and the way in which the clouds and the chiaroscuro are handled make it very similar to other early work by the painter. It shows a dune landscape near Haarlem, a subject that was also popular with other painters of the period. On the left is a hunter with a dog, hunting a rabbit. In the centre foreground, a red-coated man on a horse creates a subtle contrasting accent against the green. Behind him are some buildings and a little windmill. The sea can just be glimpsed on the horizon. Jacob borrowed one of his uncle Salomon's tricks to suggest depth: a bank of cloud running diagonally.

River View with Ferry and Bastion,
1664

Salomon Jacobsz van Ruysdael
1600/03–1670
Panel, 49.4 x 68.4 cm

The Frans Hals Museum owns several highly atmospheric river views by Salomon van Ruysdael. The painter was one of the many major and minor masters who specialized in this genre. Works like this give us a fascinating picture of the marshy countryside full of ditches, rivers and lakes that Holland always was – and in part still is. In this painting, Van Ruysdael combined an unidentified parish with a fortification, some trees and various boats on a large stretch of water. The scene centres on the ferry in the foreground: livestock and people are being taken to the other side (on the right) by a ferryman, who pulls his boat across the water with a long rope. The painter placed his signature and a date, 'SVRUYSDAEL.1664' on this ferry. There are dozens of these river views with ferry by Van Ruysdael, but he always succeeded in varying them.

The ice views with figures skating
and sledging are among the jolliest
paintings of the Golden Age. This
small panel by Isaack van Ostade is
one such piece. Young and old are
having fun on the ice, in front of an
inn. A woman in the left foreground
is selling cakes. A dog helps itself to
one of her wares. The many details
and the relaxed atmosphere of
scenes like this make them very
appealing paintings. Van Ostade
painted several of these ice scenes,
often reusing the same buildings
and figures, like the white horse
pulling the sledge (right). The artist,
who died when he was 28, was
a younger brother of the painter
Adriaen van Ostade.

Winter Landscape with Skaters,
c. 1675/1700

Salomon Gillisz Rombouts
1655–before or in 1702
Panel, 47 x 57 cm

A typical Dutch winter landscape
with skaters, one of the countless
number painted in the 17th century.
Rombouts, who came from Haarlem, placed his people skating and
sledging near a village (right) and a
castle (rear centre). In painting these
atmospheric and airy scenes, he was
following in the footsteps of fellow
natives of Haarlem like Isaack van
Ostade and Jacob van Ruisdael. One
of the earliest and best known masters in this genre was the painter
Hendrick Avercamp of Kampen.

*Mountain Landscape with Herdsmen
and Cattle at a Ford*, c. 1655/60

Nicolaes Pietersz Berchem
1621/22–1683
Panel, 75 x 108.5 cm

An everyday scene in a southern mountain region that might be in Italy, without a story or a moral: herdsmen and cattle at a ford across a river or lake. Warm golden light, space, a calm rural mood: these are the key ingredients of this virtuoso painting. With such Italian-looking, populated landscapes and harbour views, Berchem is regarded as one of the Italianate artists. He had been to Italy himself. Berchem was the son of the Haarlem still life painter Pieter Claesz, works by whom can also be found in the Frans Hals Museum's collection: painting as a trade was often passed down from father to son. Berchem left quite a diverse and, above all, extensive oeuvre of many hundreds of paintings.

The Haarlem artist Frans Post painted this tropical landscape in the
mid-17th century. It is a picture of
a place in Brazil. In the landscape,
natives (in the foreground) carry
baskets of sugar cane to a water-
powered sugar mill (left in the centre ground).

    Post went to Brazil, which was
a Dutch colony at the time, around
1640. He and Albert Eckhout had
been commissioned to record the
landscape, the inhabitants and the
fauna in drawings and paintings.
Post painted several landscapes on
the spot. After his return to Holland
in 1644, he produced a great many
more, mostly based on the many
drawings that he had made while he
was there. This painting is part of
his Dutch output. The exotic works
were highly sought after. Today
there are some 150 surviving Brazil-
ian landscapes by this artist.

Flora's Wagon of Fools,
in or shortly after 1637

Hendrick Gerritsz Pot (attributed)
c. 1580–1657
Panel, 61 x 83 cm

In this work, the painter Hendrick Pot made fun of an extraordinary phenomenon in Haarlem's history – the speculation in tulip bulbs.

The painting, which is based on a print by Crispijn van der Passe II (c. 1594-c. 1670), was made around 1640, shortly after the collapse of the speculative trade in tulips. The flower goddess Flora, under a flag adorned with tulips and holding three of the valuable blooms in her hand, is enthroned in her chariot, depicted here as a wagon of fools. Three men wearing fools' caps on their heads ride with her. *Leckebardt* (gluttony) cannot keep off the drink, *Graegrijk* (avarice) holds a bag of money and *Liegwagen* (loose talk), with a bell in his hand, tells his empty tales. Dame *Vergaeral* (col-lector's mania) weighs tulip bulbs in a set of scales (bulbs were sold by weight), and the bird of hope flies away from Dame *IJdel Hoop* (vain hope). The wagon of fools will shortly be lost at sea. The wagon is followed by a group of Haarlem weavers. They have abandoned their work, and walk behind the wagon. Haarlem weavers are known to have tried their luck in the specu-lation in tulips. The skyline of the city of Haarlem with the Church of St Bavo can be seen in the back-ground to the left.

In the 17th century tulips became
insanely popular in the Netherlands. The flower had been intro-
duced into the Netherlands from
the Turkish Empire in the 16th century. In 1635 the trade in tulips spi-
ralled, and a real tulip mania seized
the population: rich and poor alike
joined in the speculation. On 3 Feb-
ruary 1637, however, the bubble
burst. A rumour circulated that the
bulbs were worthless, prices plum-
meted, and everyone tried to sell
their bulbs.

In this painting Brueghel shows
how people had acted like foolish
monkeys. Monkeys negotiate, monkeys weigh the bulbs, monkeys
count money and monkeys keep
records. The monkey on the left has
a list of bulb prices. On the right,
a monkey pisses on tulips. Behind
him a speculator is brought before
the court for debt. A monkey sits
crying in the stocks. In the centre
background a disappointed buyer
comes to blows. On the right in the
background, a speculator is even
carried to the grave.

Jan Steen's interiors are legendary, but his outdoor scenes are equally chaotic. In this peasants' carnival, he shows peasants overindulging in drink and other things.

In the right foreground a little group of people sits smoking and drinking. On the left a man is carried away drunk, beyond lies a farmer's boy sunk in befuddled sleep. A pig, which is generally associated with gluttony and drunkenness, roots in his vomit. In the centre of the painting, musicians play, and a man, still dancing, sweeps a woman indoors with him; his intentions are evident.

Jan Steen's aim in this painting was to illustrate excess and its consequences. It is obvious that the behaviour of these peasants is objectionable. The painter has illustrated this by adding – on the far right – a woman who squats down relieving herself; a more denigrating comment on this common behaviour can hardly be conceived of.

The Haarlem artist Jacob Matham
made this large pen painting for
his prominent fellow citizen Johan
Claesz Loo, several times burgomaster and also a brewer. With pen
and ink on a prepared panel, as if
it were a large engraving, the artist
depicted two of Loo's possessions.
In the foreground is his brewery
'De Drie Leliën' on the River
Spaarne – one of the dozens of
breweries in Haarlem at the time.
In the background stands Loo's
small estate with his house
'Velserend'. In reality, it was much
further away, near the ruins of
Brederode Castle (shown in the distance) in Santpoort. Loo probably
figures twice in this work: at the

entrance to the brewery, and on the
road in front of the house. Matham
must have learnt this unusual pen
painting technique from his stepfa-
ther Hendrick Goltzius, who was
extremely accomplished in it.

*The Great Market in Haarlem
with the Church of St Bavo,
seen from the west,* 1696

Gerrit Adriaensz Berckheyde
1638–1698
Canvas, 69.5 x 90.5 cm

The Great Market and the Church of St Bavo must have been an exceptional source of inspiration to Gerrit Berckheyde; he painted this cityscape more than twenty times during his career.

This painting, which dates from 1696, provides an exact picture of the centre of Haarlem at the end of the 17th century. The majestic Church of St Bavo towers over everything. To the north of the church lies the *Vishal*, the fish market, covered to keep the smell in. On the other side of the church stands the *Vleeshal*, built in 1603, where the butchers sold their meat. It is a magnificent example of Renaissance architecture, which illustrates Haarlem's wealth in the early 17th century. In the background of the painting, it is just possible to see a part of a wooden bell tower, which was built around 1470.

Apart from the wooden bell tower and the fish market, which has been replaced by another, these buildings can still be admired in the Great Market.

The fish market takes place in the foreground of the painting, in the shadow of the Church of St Bavo. In the background the square and the town hall are bathed in bright sunlight. This strong contrast between light and shade – a characteristic feature of Gerrit Berckheyde's cityscapes – ensures a convincing effect of depth.

It was not by chance that the fish market was held by the walls of St Bavo; the shady side of the church was a good place to sell the perishable fish. The fish hall was built in 1603; it belonged to the city but was built on church land, which meant that the church shared in the income from the rental of the fish stalls. In 1796 the fish hall was replaced with a new one, built closer to the church, on the site of the former thieves' cemetery. (Thieves were not, of course, buried in the church.) The new Fish Hall is still there; it is now used as an exhibition gallery for modern art.

Interior of the Church of St Bavo
in Haarlem, looking west,
1668

Job Adriaensz Berckheyde
1630–1693
Canvas, 109.5 x 154.5 cm

The interior of the Church of St Bavo
in the Great Market in Haarlem,
looking west. Berckheyde stood in
the first bay of the choir, to the right
of the centre. St Bavo is a mainly
15th-century church and is also
known, with good reason, as the
Great Church: the choir is 45 metres
long, longer than that of famous
French cathedrals like Rheims and
Amiens. At the end of the 16th century, the Catholic Bavo Cathedral
fell into Protestant hands. The interior was stripped, and the decora-
tions were destroyed. Only a few
altarpieces survived, and they are
now in the Frans Hals Museum.
Among them are *St Luke painting
the Madonna* (p 19) and the side panels of the *Drapers' Altar* (pp 22–23)
by Maerten van Heemskerck. The
white plaster of the interior in
Berckheyde's painting recalls
'the Protestant whitewash'.

In the west window there is a
depiction of the Increasing of Arms,
a famous legendary tale of the Cru-
sades that was frequently referred
to in 17th-century Haarlem because
of the supposed heroic role of a
number of Haarlem men. We do not
know whether such a window actually existed. It may have been an
addition by the painter himself.

Job Berckheyde, like his brother
Gerrit, also painted cityscapes.

*Interior of the Church of St Anne
in Haarlem, looking from west to east,
1652*

Pieter Jansz Saenredam 1597–1665
Panel, 65.5 x 93 cm

Jacob van Campen, the architect of the Palace on the Dam in Amsterdam, designed the classical Church of St Anne (built 1646–49) for Haarlem. Van Campen's friend Pieter Saenredam devoted this work to it, as well as three other paintings and numerous drawings. The figures of the people in this bright, virtually unornamented Protestant space can also be attributed to him.

Saenredam's painting is not an exact record of the reality. The round columns were indeed designed by Van Campen, but were not all built. The interior in the painting also gives the impression of more space than is actually the case. Saenredam specialized in such hard to construct, perspectivist church views. The tranquility and the geometric clarity of his work make Saenredam's paintings instantly recognizable.

Three elegant and fashionably dressed couples sit in a garden and enjoy themselves with music, wine and one another. On the left a servant comes out of a house, bearing more drink. On the right by a fountain – in scenes like this often an allusion to fertility – there is an *etagère* on which valuable vases and dishes are displayed.

The garden party is a type of painting that seems to have been confined to Haarlem, from 1612 onwards. Esaias van de Velde, Willem Buytenwech and, rather later, Dirck Hals (p 68) were all practitioners of this genre. It was an entirely new sort of painting, very different from the art of Cornelis van Haarlem and Hendrick Goltzius that dominated the scene at this time.

These paintings, with people rolling in wealth, free of care, enjoying themselves with music and idle card games, were intended to remind the 17th-century viewer of the relativeness of earthly pleasure. Although death is not depicted here, he nonetheless looks over our shoulder. This is tellingly expressed on a print with a similar subject by Jan van de Velde: 'though we have often enjoyed great luxury, death is much closer than we know'.

Music-Making Company on a Terrace,   Dirck Franchoisz Hals 1591–1656
1620–25   Panel, 53 x 84 cm

Dirck Hals, Frans Hals's younger brother, was also a painter. He specialized in elegantly dressed 'companies'.

In this painting, a group of carefree young people give themselves over to the pleasures of life. On the right of the terrace, a small group sits making music. Behind them is a fountain – traditionally a reference to fertility – bearing a statue of Bacchus, the god of wine. On the left three men vie for the attention of a seated beauty. The two little dogs sniffing each other in the foreground make the intentions of the young men abundantly plain.

Such 'companies' usually have a moral message. They warn against overindulgence and the pursuit of earthly pleasure. Making music is meant here as an idle pastime; the pleasure of music is, after all, fleeting. The servant who stands behind the music-makers adds water to the wine and thus symbolizes moderation. And lastly, one of the young men paying court to the woman on the left stands on the box of a backgammon set: a game in which fortunes can change, as they can in love.

At first sight this is a festive scene – the partygoers play, eat and make music. But the painting has a double meaning; it warns against licentious behaviour and calls for moderation and chastity.

In the centre men and women sit around a table bearing a large dish of oysters. Oysters stood for luxury and abundance, and they also had an erotic symbolism. But caution is advised here, as the backgammon game being played on the left tells us. Because the tide can turn; at one moment it seems that you will win and the very next you have lost. So it can be with wealth – and love, which is fickle.

Music, too, had a symbolic meaning in the 17th century. When making music it is important to keep a measured beat. In the 17th century people making music in paintings were often a call to moderation.

This painting is a joint production by Dirck van Delen and Dirck Hals. Van Delen painted the Renaissance interior and Hals the figures.

Weeping, Venus bends over her
beloved Adonis. Cupid – also weeping – looks on. Adonis has been
killed by a wild boar during a hunt.
In the background, hunting dogs
continue to pursue the savage beast.

This painting illustrates a story
from the *Metamorphoses* by the
Roman author Ovid, a source on
which 17th-century artists repeat-
edly drew. The goddess Venus had
fallen in love with the beautiful
hunter Adonis and neglected her
lover, the god Mars. Enraged, Mars
set a wild boar on Adonis, intending
that the creature would kill Adonis
during the hunt. Venus had a pre-
monition about it and begged Adonis not to go hunting, but Adonis
ignored her pleas and had to pay for
this with his death.

This mythological tale was popular in the Netherlands and was
painted many times. Perhaps it
was the moral that appealed to
the Dutch; Adonis was seen as
the embodiment of reckless youth,
who brushes aside the advice of
divine love.

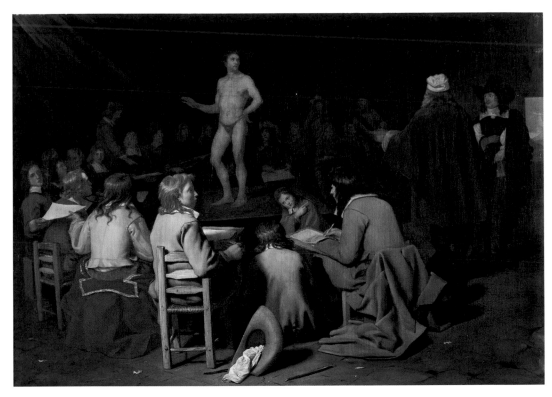

A 17th-century academy or artist's
studio: a teacher, seen from behind,
gives a group of boys a drawing lesson. Between them, in the centre,
stands a nude male model. In the
past it was thought that this was the
studio of Frans Hals and his pupils
(among them some of his sons).
However, there are no good argu-
ments to support this interpreta-
tion. This is probably not meant to
be a particular workplace but rather
a depiction of one of the phases in
the training to be an artist: drawing
from life. Other stages were copy-
ing the work of 'good masters' and
drawing plaster and marble stat-
uettes. Sweerts also devoted paintings to other phases. For some time
the artist ran his own drawing academy in Brussels.

Caring for the Children in the House
  for Destitute Children:
  Three Works of Mercy, 1663

Jan Salomonsz de Bray
1626/27–1697
Canvas, 134.5 × 154 cm

This painting was commissioned
from Jan de Bray by the Haarlem
House for Destitute Children. It
hung over the mantelpiece in the
trustees' room. The payment to
De Bray is recorded in the orphanage ledger; he received 72 guilders
for this 'picture painted by him
being 3 works of mercy'.

Of the seven Christian works
of mercy, the three depicted in this
painting relate directly to the daily
care of orphans: clothing the naked,
giving drink to the thirsty and feed-
ing the hungry. Bread is doled out,
and the children eat it hungrily, a
girl is given a drink from a tankard
(this is probably small beer, a sort
of weak beer that was drunk every
day), and all the children change
their old rags for the orphanage
clothes, recognizable by the different coloured sleeves – one red and

one black. They are helped by the
workers in the home.

The House for Destitute Children was housed in the former Convent of Mary Magdalene. The tower
in the background of the painting is
very similar to that of the convent
chapel. In 1765 the House for Destitute Children was merged with the
Heilige Geesthuis and later became
known as the Gereformeerd or
Burger Orphanage. In 1810 the
orphanage moved to the former
Old Men's Alms House, the building that now houses the Frans Hals
Museum.

This painting is a posthumous trib-ute to Frederick Henry, stadholder of the Republic of the United Provinces from 1625 to 1647. It was commissioned by the Haarlem town council in 1681 and hung in the Prinsenhof, where the stadhold-er stayed when he was in Haarlem.

Frederick Henry is crowned with laurels by Virtue. Courage, with sword and shield, stands on the other side. The Maid of Haar-lem, with the arms of Haarlem on her cloak, kneels before the stad-holder. She holds a horn of plenty, a symbol of prosperity and good for-tune. Frederick Henry is portrayed here as the commander-in-chief of the army. It was thanks to his mili-tary successes that the Eighty Years' War (1568–1648) was brought to an end by the Treaty of Münster.

The painting is not just a tribute to an important stadholder of the past. It also has a political signifi-cance. William III, a descendant of Frederick Henry and the stadholder at this time, had brought various wars to a successful conclusion and wanted to continue the fight against France. Haarlem and Rotterdam supported him in this, but Amster-dam and Leiden were opposed; they saw war as an obstacle to trade. The trade argument outweighed the rest, and there was no further fighting.

In this context, the painting can also be interpreted as a declaration of political support from the Haar-lem city government to William III; it would be war that would bring peace and prosperity, just as it had in Frederick Henry's day.

An elegantly dressed, bejewelled
young woman sits at a table. To her
right stands a chair with male attire
on it, and in the background there
is a bed – an unmistakable reference
to physical love. Other objects in
the painting make the same allusion. The lute, which has been taken
out of its case, symbolizes lost innocence. In this context, the parrot,
too, is a sexually significant motif.
The letter that the young woman
holds is undoubtedly a love letter.

The woman is engrossed in her
amorous reflections and is unaware
that death is lying in wait – she is
Vanitas incarnate. The old woman,
who to press the point home holds
a withered flower in one hand and a
skull in the other, alerts the viewer
to the transience of youthful beauty
and the brevity of life.

The Weaver's Workshop, 1656	Gillis Salomonsz Rombouts 1631–1672 Panel, 32 x 38.5 cm

This painting depicts a typical Haarlem subject: the weaver's workshop. Several Haarlem artists painted this subject, but there are no known paintings of it from any other town. It is not particularly surprising that the theme was popular in Haarlem – Haarlem was the centre of the textile trade.

In the workshop we see not only the weaver at work, but also his wife, a small baby and a toddler. An old man peers in through the window in the door. All ages are thus represented, an indication that this scene has a specific meaning. The explanation can be found in the emblemata literature of the 17th century. In his caption to the print 'the Weaver' in *Het menselyk bedryf* (1694), Jan Luyken compares human life with the weaver's shuttle:

As the shuttle flies through the warp
Thus fleeting are the days of our lives,
And they will never come again:
Let Each behave with circumspection:
As Life's web is woven Straight or ill,
So it will earn a Good or bad Wage.

A pattern of unity and good cooperation: the men strike the anvil in turn and together forge the iron.

The subject was probably taken from the emblem book by the 17th-century poet Jacob Cats. His emblems, short moralizing verses with an illustration, were often used in the 17th century. The specific emblem that has been taken as the example here bears the motto 'To forge much, one must work hard'. The poem opens with the lines:

As five or six with outstretched arms,
Strike on one anvil in mutual aid,
Thus should every man so time his stroke
That his fellow man may have his turn.

This sort of everyday scene with a moral message was popular in 17th-century Holland. The citizens who became rich in the Golden Age did not order large canvases with elevated subjects, they bought small works depicting scenes that they recognized from their everyday lives.

The grinning man refills the kitchen maid's glass. His intentions are plain: he is seducing her. His efforts will undoubtedly be successful, because the maid has already placed one foot on his knee and loosened her shift, so that her breasts are partly exposed. The scene is watched by an old man, who leans over the half-door and raises a warning finger – because this, of course, is an example of what not to do.

The shameless behaviour of the two is further emphasized by the monkey, which – chained to a block – unashamedly looks up her skirt. The monkey symbolizes man, chained to the block of his own sins.

The humorous pillorying of reprehensible behaviour on the part of kitchen maids and domestic servants in general was an almost classic subject in the 17th century, in both art and literature.

Madonna, Reading, with Child, 1622   Pieter Fransz de Grebber
c. 1600–1652/53
Panel, 98.5 x 73.4 cm

A woman sits breast-feeding her child, reading a book as she does so. Or is there more going on here? For various reasons this painting is considered to be a depiction of Mary and the infant Jesus. Firstly, at this time a simple genre scene showing a mother and child was not yet a subject being painted in Haarlem. Moreover, elements from various traditional depictions of the Madonna are combined here: the veil (virginity), reading, the giving of the breast. Even the wooden fence behind Mary has a significance in this context – it stands for the poor conditions in which Mary lived. In this painting the Roman Catholic De Grebber made a devotional work that is of a piece with the Catholic art of the time.

Between 1616 and 1639 Frans Hals painted five enormous civic guard paintings for the two Haarlem militias: the Civic Guard of St George and the Cluveniers, who were also known as the Civic Guard of St Adrian. A mammoth task, because these five canvases alone contain no fewer than 68 portraits of 61 different prominent Haarlem citizens, plus one dog.

At the time when Frans Hals painted his civic guard works, the Haarlem civic guards consisted of three different companies: the Orange, the White and the Blue Company. Each company was headed by a colonel and a provost marshal. The provost marshal (or fiscal) was responsible for money and for discipline. The officers were appointed by the town council for a period of three years. When they stepped down, they were honoured with a banquet. Three of Hals's five civic guard paintings depict just such a banquet. The officers were not eligible for immediate reappointment; they had to wait for at least three years before they could be appointed again. Each company had its own standard-bearer: the ensign. The ensigns could remain in office for as long as they were unmarried. The rank of the officers can often be deduced from the position they occupy in the painting or from their weapons.

All the able-bodied men in the city could join the civic guard provided only that they could pay for their own equipment. From 1612 onwards Frans Hals was a member of Haarlem's Civic Guard of St George. He is listed in the register of members as Frans Hals, painter, and there is a letter M by his name, which means that his weapon was a musket. Hals's membership no doubt influenced the officers in 1616 when it came to awarding the prestigious commission for the first civic guard painting.

These paintings hung in the *doelen*, the shooting ranges where the civic guards met. Both buildings still exist – the Cluveniersdoelen is now home to the Municipal Library, the St George's building has now been converted into homes, shops and offices.

There are a further twenty extant Haarlem civic guard paintings. Eighteen of them are in the Frans Hals Museum. Two were painted by Cornelis van Haarlem. Frans de Grebber painted five, as did Frans Hals, the rest were painted by other Haarlem artists.

1 Hendrick van Berckenrode (c. 1565–1634), colonel
2 Johan van Napels (1566-?), provost marshal
3 Nicolaes Woutersz van der Meer (c. 1574–1637), captain
4 Vechter Jansz van Teffelen (1563–1619), captain
5 Jacob Laurensz (c. 1560–1631), captain
6 Hugo Mattheusz Steyn (1577–1632), lieutenant
7 Cornelis Jacobsz Schout (?), lieutenant
8 Pieter Adriaensz Verbeek (?–1637), lieutenant
9 Gerrit Cornelisz Vlasman (?), ensign
10 Jacob Cornelisz Schout (?), ensign
11 Boudewijn van Offenberg (1590-?), ensign
12 servant

Hals's first civic guard painting:
the officers of the Civic Guard of
St George at their farewell banquet.
These officers served from 1612
to 1615.

Frans Hals has used a straight-
forward composition to show the
hierarchy among the officers. The
tip of the flag is the top of an imaginary pyramid within which the officers are ranged. On the left at the
head of the table sits the colonel,
with the provost marshal on his
right. They are the highest-ranking
officers. Then come the three captains and finally the three lieutenants. Around them stand the
three ensigns and the servant.
Ensigns, usually young men of
good family, were the only members
to stay for longer than three years;
they could keep their position as
long as they were unmarried. Two
ensigns in this painting, Boudewijn
van Offenberg and Jacob Schout,
were still ensigns in 1627, and also
appear in the painting of the Civic
Guard of St George dating from
1627 (pp 84–85). The ensigns carry
the flags of the Civic Guard of
St George, blue and yellow chequers
at the top, and red and white stripes
at the bottom, with the arms of
Haarlem in the centre.

The seated captain in the foreground is Nicolaes van der Meer.
Frans Hals painted his portrait again
in 1631, together with that of his
wife, Cornelia Vooght (pp 98–99).

*Banquet of the Officers of
the Civic Guard of St George,* 1624–27

Frans Hals *c.* 1582–1666
Canvas, 179 x 257.5 cm

The officers who served in the Civic
Guard of St George from 1624 to
1627 attend their farewell banquet.
Officers were appointed for three
years by the town council. The end
of their term of office was marked
with a banquet.

The officers and ensigns wear
sashes in the colours of their company: white, orange or blue. The
place of honour, in the foreground
and at the head of the table, is
occupied by the colonel, Aernout
Druyvesteyn. A place in the foreground is also reserved for Ensign
Boudewijn van Offenberg (8), Captain Michiel de Wael (2) and Captain
Nicolaes le Febure (3). It was these
men who in 1625 had taken part in
an expedition of both Haarlem civic
guards to Heusden in North Bra-
bant to provide reinforcements.
Their participation in this 'action'
may have prompted the commis-
sioning of this group portrait. The
officers of the Cluveniers also had
a civic guard portrait painted at the
end of this period of office.

Captain Le Febure (3) is shown
standing so that it is not obvious
just how short he was. Boudewijn
van Offenberg (8) and Jacob Schout
(10) are also portrayed in the civic
guard portrait of 1616 (pp 82–83).
They were standard-bearers from
1612 to 1627.

1 Aernout Druyvesteyn (1577–1627), colonel
2 Michiel de Wael (1596–1659), captain
3 Nicolaes le Febure (1589–1641), captain
4 Nicolaes Verbeek (1582–1637), captain
5 Cornelis Boudewijns (c. 1587–1635), lieutenant
6 Frederick Coning (1594–1636), lieutenant
7 Jacob Olycan (1596–1638), lieutenant
8 Boudewijn van Offenberg (1590-?), ensign
9 Dirck Dicx (1603 ?), ensign
10 Jacob Schout (?-?), ensign
11 Arent Jacobsz Koets (?–1635), servant

Banquet of the Officers
of the Civic Guard of St Adrian
(the Cluveniers), 1624–27

Frans Hals
c. 1582–1666
Canvas, 183 x 266.5 cm

'Very well handled from life,' wrote the Haarlem city historian Samuel Ampzing of this civic guard painting in his *Beschrijvinge van de stad Haarlem* of 1628.

The painting portrays the eleven officers of the Cluveniers at their farewell banquet. In the background stands the servant, Willem Ruychaver. On the left at the head of the table sits the colonel, Willem Claesz Vooght. He can be recognized by his orange sash. Next to him sits the fiscal, Johan Damius, who is being handed a glass. The composition of the painting is balanced and carefully thought out. The members of the civic guard are divided into two groups linked in the composition by the officer with the knife: he belongs to the group on the right, but looks to the left.

The position of officer in the civic guard was an honorary unpaid post. These posts were reserved for a small group of influential, well-to-do Haarlem citizens. In Haarlem, the owners of prosperous breweries were among the wealthiest people in the city. Captain Willem Warmont (3) was the owner of the brewery known as 't Gecroonde Ancker, Captain Johan Schatter (4) owned the brewery De Gecroonde Ruyt and Ensign Loth Schout (10) owned De Twee Gecroonde Starren.

Fiscal Johan Damius (2) was a physician, Lieutenant Outgert Akersloot (7) a goldsmith. On the far left stands Ensign Adriaen

1 Willem Claesz Vooght (1572–1630), colonel
2 Johan Damius (?–1648), fiscal
3 Willem Warmont (1583–1649), captain
4 Johan Schatter (1594–1673), captain
5 Gilles de Wildt (1576–1630), captain
6 Nicolaes van Napels (c. 1598–1630), lieutenant
7 Outgert Akersloot (1576–1636), lieutenant
8 Matthijs Haeswindius (1588–1631), lieutenant
9 Adriaen Matham (c. 1599–1660), ensign
10 Loth Schout (1600–1655), ensign
11 Pieter Ramp (c. 1592-c. 1660), ensign
12 Willem Ruychaver (c. 1563–1634), servant

Matham (9), draughtsman and engraver. In 1634 he was a witness at the baptism of Frans Hals's daughter Suzanna. A striking note is the dog at his feet; this is the only dog in any of the Haarlem civic guard portraits.

*Meeting of Officers and Sergeants
of the Civic Guard of St Adrian
(the Cluveniers)*, 1633

Frans Hals
c. 1582–1666
Canvas, 207 x 337 cm

Officers and sergeants of the Cluveniers meeting outdoors. The highest in rank are positioned in the foreground: the colonel, captains and lieutenants. The sergeants are allocated a place behind the table; this is the first time that Frans Hals also portrayed non-commissioned officers.

The two groups in the composition are linked by Lieutenant Jacob Buttinga (5) centre, in front of the table. He belongs to the group on the left, with the colonel as the central point, but turns to Van der Horn, who is at the centre of the right-hand group.

The officers of the guard carry the weapons that accompany their posts: the colonel leans on his commander's staff, the captains carry pikes with tassels, and the sergeants have halberds. Captain Johan Schatter (2) had been a captain in the Cluveniers before. He is also depicted in the civic guard portrait of the Cluveniers dating from 1627 (pp 86–87). Colonel Johan Claesz Loo (1) and Lieutenant Hendrick Gerritsz Pot (7) both also appear in the civic guard portrait of 1639 (pp 90–91).

The painting must originally have been much more colourful. This is particularly evident in the trees in the background: they were once green but have discoloured to brown over the centuries.

*Officers and Sergeants
of the Civic Guard of St George*, 1639

Frans Hals *c.* 1582–1666
Canvas, 218 x 421 cm

This civic guard portrait illustrates yet again how the important posts in the city rotated among a few prominent, wealthy families. Colonel Johan Claesz Loo (1) owned the brewery De Drie Leliën and was also a member of Haarlem town council. From 1630 to 1633 he was colonel of the Cluveniers (pp 88–89). Sergeant Nicolaes Loo (16) was the colonel's son. He also had a brewery: 't Hoeffijser. The colonel's son-in-law, Florens van der Hoef (4), was a captain. He was a councillor, sheriff and burgomaster, and held various posts in the civic guard. Captain Nicolaes Grauwert (5) was the colonel's brother-in-law. He, similarly, was a councillor and sheriff.

Tradition has it that the second figure from the left in the back row (19) is Frans Hals himself. It is true that Hals had been a member of the civic guard since 1612, but ordinary members never appeared in civic guard portraits. It would therefore have been an extraordinary privilege if this is indeed a portrait of Frans Hals. Perhaps he was allowed to give himself a place amidst the officers and sergeants because he had already painted five large group portraits of the civic guard.

*Regents of St Elizabeth's
Hospital in Haarlem*, 1641

Frans Hals c. 1582–1666
Canvas, 153 x 252 cm
On loan from the Elisabeth
van Thüringenfonds

Five male trustees of St Elizabeth's
Hospital sit around the table in the
trustees' room. St Elizabeth's Hospital, the hospital for the poor, was
located in Groot Heiligland, oppo-
site the present day Frans Hals
Museum. These regents were
appointed for a year.

From left to right are Siewert
Sem Warmont, Salomon Cousaert,
Johan van Clarenbeeck (secretary,
shown with a book), Dirck Dircksz
Del (president) and François Wou-
ters (identifiable as the treasurer by
the coins on the table in front of
him). The regents are dignified and
serious, they are dressed soberly in
black, in accordance with the fash
ion and as appropriate to their position in a charitable institution. The
map hanging on the wall in the
background may allude to one of the
duties of the trustees of the hospital: they managed the land owned
by the hospital.

St Elizabeth's Hospital also
had four female trustees. Their portraits were also painted in 1641, by
Johannes Verspronck (pp 106–107).
These two regents' portraits of 1641
by Hals and Verspronck were the
first ever painted in Haarlem.

The Old Men's Alms House was
a home where men over the age of
sixty could spend their declining
years. The home opened its doors
to the first residents in 1609. The
building, in Groot Heiligland, still
exists and is now the Frans Hals
Museum. In 1664 Frans Hals painted the portraits of the regents and
regentesses who made up the board
of trustees of the Old Men's Alms
House in that year.

The regents sit around a table
covered with a dark red tablecloth.
The housefather stands on the right
in the background. He and the
housemother were responsible for
the day to day running of the institution.

Hals's less than precise manner
of painting – characteristic of his
later work – provoked great criti-
cism in the 19th century. It was said
that he was too old to paint. Frans
Hals was over eighty when he made
this portrait. The second regent
from the right has an odd look in
his eyes. In the 19th century it was
thought that he had been portrayed
drunk, but nowadays experts
believe that he was suffering from
facial paralysis.

*Regentesses of
the Old Men's Alms House*, 1664

Frans Hals c. 1582–1666
Canvas, 170.5 x 249.5 cm

The four regentesses who were part of the board of trustees of the Old Men's Alms House in 1664 were Adriaentje Schouten, Marijtje Willems, Anna van Damme and Adriana Bredenhoff. They are portrayed, with the housemother, in this group portrait by Frans Hals. The painting in the background may be of the Good Samaritan, a subject that illustrates the charity of the regentesses.

The portraits of the regentesses and the regents have been both admired and reviled over the centuries – admired for the manner of their painting, which had a particularly marked impact on the Impressionists and Realists of the 19th century, and reviled because people thought that the portraits of the regentesses were not very flattering.

For a long time it was believed that Frans Hals had lived in the Old Men's Alms House. It was said that this portrait of the regentesses and that of the regents were his way of taking his revenge on the strict trustees. But Frans Hals never lived in the Old Men's Alms House. We do, however, know that in the 1630s Frans Hals and his large family lived in Groot Heiligland, the street where the Old Men's Alms House stood.

Portrait of Nicolaes Woutersz
van der Meer, 1631
Portrait of Cornelia Claesdr Vooght,
1631

Frans Hals *c.* 1582–1666
Panel, 128 x 100.5 cm

Panel, 126.5 x 101 cm

Nicolaes van der Meer and Cornelia
Vooght were a prominent Haarlem
couple. Van der Meer (*c.* 1574–1637)
was a brewer, sheriff, burgomaster
on more than one occasion and an
officer of the civic guard. In his post
of captain he was also painted by
Frans Hals in the civic guard portrait
of 1616 (pp 82–83). The couple were
portrayed in two separate paintings,
which belong together. The wall
in one portrait appears to continue
through into the other. Traditionally the portrait of the man hangs on
the left and that of the woman on
the right. In the course of his long
career, Frans Hals painted many of
these pendant portraits of men and
women.

There is something strange
going on with these two portraits.
X-rays have revealed that the faces
of Nicolaes and Cornelia have been
painted over the top of other portraits. We do not know why this
was done. Perhaps the sitters were
not satisfied or became dissatisfied
with their portraits; perhaps later
owners (the portraits remained in
the family for a long time) had the
portraits altered.

The coats of arms in the two
paintings are also later additions,
probably 19th century. The Prussian
blue pigment used in the coats of
arms was not in general use until
after 1720, and the arms are not in
evidence on a drawing after the portrait of Cornelia Vooght made by
Johan van der Sprang in 1762.

For many years the portrait of
Zaffius was thought to be the earliest known painting by Frans Hals.
Nowadays the attribution to Hals is
disputed on stylistic grounds. Frans
Hals has a recognizable style, he is
known for his assured and sponta-
neous brushwork. This portrait of
Jacobus Zaffius, although it is a good
portrait, does not display this style.

Jacobus Zaffius was the highest
official in the Catholic Church
in Haarlem. He was provost and
archdeacon. Haarlem had been
a Reformed city since 1578, and
Catholicism was officially banned.
But the town council turned a blind
eye, and Zaffius was able to continue in his post.

In 1630 Jan van de Velde II made
an engraving of the portrait of
Zaffius. Below the print is the legend 'Frans Hals pinxit' (Frans Hals
painted this). In the print Zaffius is
shown from the waist up. His hand
rests on a skull. Because the print
shows more than the painting, it
was thought that the painting was
originally larger, but this is not the
case. Technical examination of the
material of the panel has revealed
that it has never been cut down. The
print and this painting were probably both made after a now lost original by Frans Hals.

This work was painted by Judith Leyster, the first female painter in Haarlem. She was probably a pupil of Frans Hals, and her paintings are similar to his in both style and subject.

Grinning broadly, a man holds up a tankard. He is Pekelharing, a stage character who cropped up in the farces of the time. His name means 'salt herring', a Dutch speciality that causes a raging thirst, and he was a true drunkard. Pekelharing was often featured in paintings; he is to be found, for instance, in a work by Frans Hals, also painted around 1629.

Judith Leyster's Pekelharing was guilty not just of drinking, but of smoking too. On the table on the left stands a burning stove; alongside it lie a pipe, a paper of tobacco and some splinters of wood to light the pipe. In this period, alcohol and tobacco were seen as great threats to mankind.

A whole family has had itself portrayed making music. A girl plays
a cithern, beside her stands a boy
with a violin, then a lute-player,
a singer and a cellist. In front of the
cello lie music parts, for the bass and
the tenor.

This is not just a family portrait;
the painting is crammed with symbolism. Making music together
symbolizes the harmony in the
family. Other symbols of harmony
are the two clasped hands and the
burning heart with two arrows on
the harpsichord. The little dog on
the cushion symbolizes fidelity.
Moderation is important to a harmonious family life: the clock and
the young singer beating time are
allusions to this. On the right stands
a little boy blowing bubbles. In one
hand he holds a dish of soapy water
(a shell on a stick), in the other a
bubble pipe. Children blowing bubbles in 17th-century paintings are
reminders of the brevity of life. The
boy may already have been dead
when this family portrait was painted. There are other deceased members of the family portrayed in this
painting – in paintings within the
painting. One of the men behind
the harpsichord, for instance, holds
a small oval portrait in his hand,
probably a miniature of his late wife.

Portrait of Anthonie
Charles de Liedekercke, 1637

Portrait of Willemina van Braeckel,
1637

Johannes Cornelisz Verspronck
1601/03–1662
Canvas, 84 x 66.5 cm
Canvas, 84 x 66.5 cm

Like Frans Hals, the other great portrait painter in Haarlem, Johannes Verspronck, concentrated on painting portraits, but their styles are very different. Verspronck usually worked very meticulously with great attention to detail; Frans Hals's manner was much freer. Both painters were very popular and were given many commissions by patrons in Haarlem and elsewhere.

Anthonie Charles de Liedekercke (1587–1661) and Willemina van Braeckel (1604/05–after 1661) married in Amsterdam in 1627. Ten years later they had their portraits painted by Johannes Verspronck. Anthonie de Liedekercke, born in Antwerp, was a naval captain and the States General's envoy in Morocco in 1640–41. After their marriage the couple settled in Haarlem. In 1638 they had a son, Samuel. He can be found with his parents in the portrait by Gerard ter Borch (p. 108).

The well-to-do couple have dressed in their finery for their portraits. Willemina van Braeckel's dress is made of costly fabrics and lace. In her hand she holds an ostrich-feather fan, an important status symbol at the time. Her husband is clad in stately black. They both wear large lace ruffs.

The coats of arms in the paintings were added later, probably in the 18th century.

The four regentesses of St Elizabeth's Hospital had their portraits painted by Johannes Verspronck in 1641. The regents had their portraits painted in the same year by Frans Hals, the other great Haarlem portrait painter (pp 92–93).

The regentesses sit at a table as if they are holding a meeting. The ledger, the slate with a piece of chalk, and the inkstand and pens are attributes that refer to their work as trustees of the Hospital; they were responsible for the administration and for the organization of the housekeeping, and they supervised the female staff. The ward can be seen through an open door on the right. Beside the bed stands a stick, used by the patient in getting in and out of bed. A sconce hangs on the wall.

We know the names of these women. They are Guertge Laurensdr, Belitge van Schilperoordt, Elisabeth van Teffelen and Beatrix Schatter. Unfortunately, we do not know for certain which name belongs to which woman. The regentesses wear sober, dark clothes. By 1640 the large millstone ruffs were already rather outmoded and only older women still wore them. These women are all getting on in years. The youngest are Elisabeth van Teffelen and Beatrix Schatter. They were born in 1584, so that they were well into their fifties when this portrait was painted.

*Portrait of Anthonie
Charles de Liedekercke,
his wife Willemina van Braeckel
and their son Samuel, c.* 1650–55

Gerard ter Borch 1617–1681
Panel, 45 x 39 cm

In 1637 Johannes Verspronck portrayed Anthonie Charles de Liedekercke (1587–1661) and Willemina van Braeckel (1604/05–after 1661) as a prosperous couple (pp 104–105). In 1638 their son Samuel was born. Some fifteen years later they had their portraits painted again, this time with their son.

In this portrait by Ter Borch, De Liedekercke was over 65, the much younger Willemina was about fifty. Their son, who must have been about sixteen, looks delicate and fragile. Samuel enrolled as a law student at the University of Leiden on 7 May 1654, but died shortly afterwards. It is quite possible that the boy's death was the reason for this family portrait. The closed watch Samuel's mother holds out to him could be conceived as a reference to his death.

Ter Borch's subdued and rather melancholy portrait contrasts sharply with the portraits that Verspronck painted. In those, the florid De Liedekercke and his wife, wearing magnificent clothes and costly jewellery, presented themselves as rich, prosperous people. In this later portrait they are soberly dressed. Samuel's elegant outfit, however, is much more opulent and fashionable. He wears a short open doublet, from under which emerge pink ribbons, and a long grey cloak trimmed with gold braid.

Self-portrait, c. 1665

Job Adriaensz Berckheyde
1630–1693
Panel, 52 x 40 cm

In the second half of the 1650s, Job Berckheyde and his brother Gerrit went on a study trip to Germany. Among the places they visited was Heidelberg where, according to the 18th-century artists' biographer Arnold Houbraken, the brothers each painted Elector Karl Ludwig of the Palatinate's hunting party. The elector was delighted with the paintings, accepted them and rewarded the brothers with a medallion.

The gold medallion that Job wears on his chest, suspended on a broad ribbon, in this self-portrait may be the medallion about which Houbraken goes into so much detail. The portrait was probably painted shortly after the brothers' return to Haarlem. Berckheyde wears dark clothes with a flat collar and tassels. He has a beret on the back of his head.

An interesting note is that this self-portrait can be seen as a painting within a painting in another self-portrait by Job Berckheyde, now in the Uffizi in Florence. In the Uffizi portrait the painter is in his studio, wearing clothes that were old-fashioned for the time, and possibly never really existed as such. He is surrounded by attributes that symbolize the senses. The self-portrait hangs on the back wall of the studio and is shown – frame and all – in mirror image.

*The Regents of
the Leper Hospital in Haarlem,*1667

Jan Salomonsz de Bray
1626/27–1697
Canvas, 141 x 197.5 cm

Like many other cities, Haarlem had a lepers' hospital, which cared for people with leprosy, plague or other infectious diseases. The Leper Hospital was outside the city because of the danger of infection. Jan de Bray painted the regents and regentesses of this institution in 1667.

After the deaths of Johannes Verspronck (in 1662) and Frans Hals (in 1666), De Bray became the leading portrait painter in Haarlem. He had already proved himself a worthy successor to the two great masters in 1663, the year he painted the portraits of the regents and regentesses of the Haarlem orphanage. His bold compositions and lively figures obviously appealed to the trustees of the institutions.

The three male trustees of the Leper Hospital are shown seated at a table, engaged in their administrative duties: keeping the books and managing the money. A valuable Indian carpet covers the table. The vitality of the scene is created because it has been made to appear as if the housefather has just come in with a new patient. He hands one of the regents a piece of paper, a certificate of infection that was drawn up by a surgeon and entitled the patient to be admitted to the hospital. The boy's head is bald and covered in sores, a symptom of his disease.

*The Regentesses of
the Leper Hospital in Haarlem*, 1667

Jan Salomonsz de Bray
1626/27–1697
Canvas, 142 x 197.5 cm

The three regentesses were
responsible for the administration
and for the organization of the
housekeeping, and they supervised
the female staff. On the table lie the
attributes appropriate to their posts:
money, a ledger, an inkstand. The
woman on the right is the housemother, who was responsible, with
the housefather, for the day to day
running of the Leper Hospital.

The names of the regents and
regentesses who were in office in
1667 are known, but it has not been
possible to link them to the individ-
ual men and women in the portraits.

Kitchen Scene, c. 1620/25

Floris Gerritsz van Schooten
1585/88–1656
Panel, 91.4 x 155 cm

A woman stands in a kitchen, gutting a fish, while a child offers her a flower to smell. Various foods lie on the table in front of her. On this side of the table a cat sniffs a fish, while a mouse scavenges under the cooking pot on the right. In the background a woman stands by the fire, stirring a pan.

The fish, the pieces of meat, the poultry, the vegetables are all depicted individually, in their entirety. The table is shown from slightly above, so that the items of food do not overlap, but are painted one above the other. This was the usual practice in still life painting at this time. Over the next twenty years, the vantage point would become lower and lower, and the objects would increasingly overlap, so that these scenes looked more and more realistic.

Often 17th-century paintings, particularly still lifes, had a moral message or a deeper significance. It is not clear whether the motif of the child holding a flower for the woman to smell is meant to convey anything deeper or more significant than the simple fact that a flower smells better than a fish.

They look real – the crumbling
cheeses, the apples, the glass of
wine, the trailing apple peel, the
dully gleaming pewter plate. Floris
van Dijck shows us that he was a
past master at rendering different
materials. In the 17th century
Schrevelius put it like this, 'Here
you have Floris van Dijck, who
could lure and catch the eager
women, indeed the very birds
with his artistic brush'.

Various meanings have been
ascribed to this still life in the past.
It is certainly no coincidence that
the various items of food in the
painting represent the four flavours:
the apples are sour, the nuts bitter,
the cheeses salt and the grapes
sweet. The two stacked cheeses also
call to mind an old Dutch saying,
'put butter with cheese and the
devil you'll please'. Two items of
dairy products on top of one another, usually butter and cheese, were
seen as extravagance. This still life
can thus be interpreted as an admo-
nition to sobriety – something that
would have held particular appeal
for the Calvinist Dutch of the time.

It is no longer possible to discov-
er whether the painter actually
intended to embody this message
in the painting. It is equally likely
that he simply painted a customary
combination of foodstuffs. And as
far as the large cheeses, so prominently displayed, are concerned –
cheese was an important Dutch
export even in the 17th century.

'Equid sunt aliud, quam breve gaudium?' Or in translation, 'What are these other than a brief joy?' The viewer of this still life is asked to ponder this philosophical question.

All the objects in this painting allude to the transience of earthly things. The skull and the thighbone beside it signify death. The fly on the forehead stands for the persistence with which death pursues us. The books refer to the inadequacy of human knowledge. Flowers are symbolic of the brevity of life, since they bloom for such a short time. The valuable exotic shell, the pearls and the coins are reminders that earthly riches are vain in the face of death.

But there is a ray of light in the darkness, as the French proverb written on the paper protruding from the book tells us – 'mourir pour vivre', die to live, a reference to life after death, the only life that is worthwhile. The butterfly is also an allusion to this hopeful prospect: the butterfly lived as a caterpillar, to become a butterfly. Thus, the human spirit, when it leaves this earthly life, will find salvation.

'Flowerpots' is what flower still lifes were apparently disrespectfully called in the 17th century. Nonetheless, these little paintings were extremely popular and much sought-after by the art-loving public.

This flower still life by Bollongier, the Haarlem specialist in this genre, depicts a pink and red paeony, two tulips, an orange and red lily, a red and white carnation and white primulas. The arrangement of the flowers in the vase looks somewhat unnatural; the large tulip at the back makes the whole thing rather top-heavy. Nevertheless, the bouquet is entirely in accordance with the 17th-century rules for the art of flower arranging. According to a treatise by Giovanni Battista Ferrari dating from 1633, a good bouquet is characterized by a compact arrangement in the shape of a cone, with the most beautiful or rarest flower crowning the whole. In this painting the crowning glory is a 'Semper Augustus', the emperor among tulips, which in the days of tulip mania could fetch thousands of guilders – and thus is rightly at the top (pp 57–59).

It is not inconceivable that the painting evoked thoughts of mortality in the 17th-century viewer. The petals of the large tulip are curling, and a small petal has already dropped; this tulip – however costly – does not have eternal life. Moreover, a snail crawls across the table. This is a commonplace creature that reminds man of his place.

This still life has been called 'a monochrome banquet'; 'monochrome' because of the restricted palette – Pieter Claesz used only brown, ochre and olive – and 'banquet' because of the depiction of the laden table. These still lifes were very much sought-after in the 1630s and 1640s, and a great many Haarlem people owned one.

In this still life there are three pewter plates, one holding oysters, another bread, while a large crab lies on the third plate at the back. On the right is a large rummer filled with wine. On the left is a silver salt cellar containing large grains of salt. Between the plates lies a paper cone of peppercorns.

The painter was concerned not only with showing different materials in juxtaposition, but also with capturing the reflection of the light. Here Pieter Claesz uses white highlights to make his objects shine: the points on the glass and the glass itself, the edges of the oyster shells, the grains of salt on the salt cellar, the grapes and the tips of the crab's pincers.

From 1640 onwards, Heda's still lifes became ever more crowded. In the 1630s his compositions were still relatively simple. Then, in the 1640s, the fashion for more sumptuous still lifes developed in Holland – extravagant paintings with a great variety of objects. The artistic challenge for the painter was no longer solely to render materials with deceptive realism, but also to place a great variety of objects in a harmonious composition. Heda went with the times, and also started to paint these sumptuous still lifes. In this – still comparatively simple – piece, he reveals himself to be an accomplished master of the genre.

Heda is sometimes described as the master of reflection. In this painting he has taken full advantage of the reflective qualities of shiny materials. In the silver jug, for instance, we can see the reflections not only of a window but also of the nautilus shell cup and the crab. The glazing bars of a window frame are reflected in the wine glass next to it. The pewter plate on the left reflects the porcelain plate, while the plate on the right shows the reflection of the crab lying on it.

Still Life with Dead Birds, 1659

Salomon Jacobsz van Ruysdael
1600/03–1670
Panel, 43 x 36 cm

There are nine known still lifes by
the landscape painter Salomon van
Ruysdael, uncle of the more famous
Jacob. Most of them show dead
birds; one of them is a still life with
fish. The works are all dated and
were made in the period 1659–62,
when the painter was around sixty
years old. During this time Van
Ruysdael continued to paint landscapes. This panel depicts a wicker
basket containing dead finches,
blackbirds and song thrushes. At
this time, songbirds were caught
with nets and lime, and were eaten.

Vanitas Still Life with the Portrait of the Artist, c. 1660

Vincent Laurensz van der Vinne
1628–1702
Canvas, 107.8 x 91.9 cm

This creates a rather untidy impression. A great many different objects lie piled up on a table – they are all vanitas symbols. A large, battered book, a celestial globe and other scientific instruments, including compasses, a pair of spectacles and a urinal, point to the imperfection and transience of human knowledge. A lute and two flutes remind the viewer that music gives only fleeting pleasure. The painting also contains several symbols that refer more generally to mortality, such as the hourglass, bubbles and a death's head. The death's head is crowned with a laurel wreath, and the legend reads in translation, 'the end crowns the work'.

Over the edge of the table hangs a sheet of paper bearing the likeness of the artist himself. This drawing, made by his friend Leendert van der Cooghen, still exists. By adding his own portrait to a vanitas still life, Vincent van der Vinne gives his painting an additional message: everything that is earthly and human is transient, but art is eternal, and the artist is immortalized by his art.

BIBLIOGRAPHY

The entries in this guide are based on the as yet unpublished catalogue of the collection of 16th- and 17th-century art, and include contributions by P. Biesboer, J.M. Bloemsma, M.W. van Dam, E. Hendriks, N. Köhler, K. Levy-van Halm, E.R. Runia, A. Seidenkranz, B.C. Sliggers, I. van Thiel-Stroman, P.J.J. van Thiel, J.E. Torringa, W. van de Watering.

I. VAN BEEK-MULDER, M. POL-MAN, *De Hallen in Haarlem, De Vis- Vlees- en Verweyhal op de Grote Markt in Haarlem*, Zwolle 1993

T. VAN BUEREN, *'De beste schilders van het gantsche Nederlandt'. Karel van Mander en de Haarlemse schilderkunst*, The Hague 1994 (Openbaar Kunstbezit I)

T. VAN BUEREN, *Tot lof van Haarlem: Het beleid van de stad Haarlem ten aanzien van de kunstwerken uit de geconfisqueerde geestelijke instellingen*, Hilversum 1993

M. CARASSO-KOK, J. LEVY-VAN HALM (ed.), *Schutters in Holland: Kracht en zenuwen van de stad*, Haarlem (Frans Hals Museum) 1988

Catalogue *The Golden Age of the seventeenth century. Dutch painting from the collection of the Frans Hals Museum*, Osaka (The National Museum of Art) 1988

Catalogue *De trots van Haarlem*, Haarlem (Frans Hals Museum and Teylers Museum) 1995

A. VAN DIEPEN, H.C. FUHRI SNETHLAGE, *Haarlem en Hals: een stad en zijn schilder*, Zwolle/Haarlem 1990

RUDOLF E.O. EKKART, *Johannes Cornelisz. Verspronck. Leven en werken van een Haarlems portretschilder uit de 17de eeuw*, Haarlem 1979

N. KÖHLER, K. LEVY-VAN HALM, *Frans Hals, Schuttersstukken*, Maarssen/Den Haag 1990

CAREL VAN MANDER, *Het Schilder-Boeck waer in voor eerst de leerlustighe ieught den grondt der edel vry schilderconst in verscheyden deelen wort voorghedraghen. Daer nae in dry deelen t'leven der vermaerde doorluchtighe schilders des ouden, en nieuwen tyds. Eyntlyck d'wtlegghinghe op den* Metamorphoseon *Pub. Ouïdij Nasonis. Oock daerbeneffens wtbeeldinghe der figueren. Alles dienstich en nut den schilders constbeminders en dichters, oock allen staten van menschen*, Haarlem 1604 (2nd edition, Amsterdam 1618)

N. MIDDELKOOP, A. VAN GREVENSTEIN, *Frans Hals. Leven, werken, restauratie*, Amsterdam 1988

M. POLMAN, *Het Frans Halsmuseum: van Oudemannenhuis tot kunsttempel. Bouwgeschiedenis en rondwandeling*, Haarlem 1990 (Haarlemse miniaturen 21)

G.F. VAN DER REE-SCHOLTENS et al. (ed.), *Deugd boven geweld. Een geschiedenis van Haarlem, 1245–1995*, Hilversum 1995

G. SCHWARTZ, M.J. BOK, *Pieter Saenredam. De schilder in zijn tijd*, Maarssen/The Hague 1989

S. SLIVE et al., *Frans Hals*, Washington (National Gallery of Art), London (Royal Academy of Arts), Haarlem (Frans Hals Museum) 1990

P.J.J. VAN THIEL, *Cornelis Cornelisz van Haarlem 1562–1638. A Monograph and Catalogue Raisonné*, Doornspijk 1999 (Aetas Aurea XIII)

Authors:
  Antoon Erftemeijer
  Henriëtte Fuhri Snethlage
  Neeltje Köhler
Editing:
  Henriëtte Fuhri Snethlage
Translation:
  Lynne Richards
Photographs:
  Tom Haartsen
Design:
  Antoon De Vylder,
  Herentals, België
Typesetting:
  De Diamant Pers nv,
  Herentals, België
Printing:
Die Keure nv, Bruges, Belgium
ISBN 90-76588-54-6
NUR 643

No part of this publication may be reproduced and/or published in print, photocopy, microfilm or any other form without prior permission from the publisher.

© 2003 Ludion, Amsterdam-Ghent and Frans Hals Museum, Haarlem
© 2003 Photography

Instituut Collectie Nederland
Berckheyde, Gerrit Adriaensz *The Great Market in Haarlem with the Church of St Bavo seen from the west,* 1696
Hals, Dirck *Music-Making Company on a Terrace,* 1620/25
Hals, Dirck en Delen, Dirck van *Festive Company in a Renaissance Room,* 1628
Heda, Willem Claesz *Still Life with Pie and Silver Jug,* 1658
Molenaer, Jan Miense *Family Making Music,* ca 1635
Mostaert, Jan *Episode from the Conquest of America, c.* 1540
Pot, Hendrick Gerritsz *Allegory on Transience, c.* 1633
Rijksmuseum, Amsterdam
Leyster, Judith Jansdr *The Jolly Toper,* 1629
Mauritshuis, Den Haag
Cornelisz van Haarlem, Cornelis *The Marriage of Peleus and Thetis,* 1592/93
Cornelisz van Haarlem, Cornelis *The Massacre of the Innocents,* 1591
Goltzius, Hendrick Jansz *Hercules and Cacus,* 1613

Goltzius, Hendrick Jansz *Mercurius,* 1611
Goltzius, Hendrick Jansz *Minerva,* 1611
Heemskerck, Maerten van *Side panels of the Drapers' Altar:* outside *the Annunciation,* inside *the Adoration of the Shepherds and the Adoration of the Magi,* 1546/47
Elisabeth van Thüringenfonds, Haarlem
Hals, Frans *Regents of St Elizabeth's Hospital,* 1641
Verspronck, Johannes *The Regentesses of St Elizabeth's Hospital in Haarlem,* 1641